Catholics
SPENDING
and
Acting
Justly

Catholics Spending and Acting Justly offers a clear but challenging "see, judge, and act" process for small groups to use in response to the economic challenges of everyday life. If taken seriously, this small booklet could change our lives, our communities, and our world.

Marie Dennis
Director
Maryknoll Office for Global Concerns

An excellent resource for Catholic parishes and organizations, especially at a time of economic crisis. A prominent economist steeped in Catholic social teaching and spirituality inspires Catholics to better integrate their faith into their everyday economic choices. A rare resource indeed!

Gerard Powers
Director of Catholic Peacebuilding
Kroc Institute for International Peace Studies
University of Notre Dame

This is an inspiring and practical study guide that brings to life the riches of Catholic social teaching. It helps Catholics move from theory to concrete action by applying Church teaching to the economic realities of our everyday lives.

Ron Krietemeyer
Director for Poverty Education
Catholic Charities of St. Paul and Minneapolis

Catholics SPENDING and Acting Justly

A Small-Group Guide for Living Economic Stewardship

Charles K. Wilber

ave maria press AMP notre dame, indiana

© 2011 by Charles K. Wilber

Founded in 1865, Ave Maria Press is a ministry of the United States Province of Holy Cross.

www.avemariapress.com

ISBN-10 1-59471-258-1   ISBN-13 978-1-59471-258-6

Cover and text design by Andy Wagoner.

Printed and bound in the United States of America.

Contents

Preface

What are we Roman Catholic Christians to do when we encounter financial difficulties or when our nation's economy weakens? Do we suffer in silence or grumble to those immediately around us? Do we watch others suffer and do nothing? Do we lose hope? And, perhaps most importantly, should our behavior during tough times be all that different from our economic behavior during boom times? This little book will help introduce you to basic economics, to Catholic social teaching, and to the observe-judge-act small-group method so that you might be better equipped to answer these questions. I hope it will also teach you how to engage in the necessary conversations about how you spend your money, time, energy, and other precious resources all of the time, not just during times of economic distress. This booklet is designed to help you become a faithful steward of our global economy now and for the rest of your life.

Christ has no body now on earth but yours, no hands but yours, no feet but yours. Yours are the eyes through which Christ's compassion is to look out to the earth, yours are the feet by which he is to go about doing good, and yours are the hands by which he is to bless us now.

—Saint Teresa of Avila

During the late 1950s, my wife and I became very involved in our local parish, particularly in its social ministry. It was then that our Christian faith became revitalized as we came to realize through study of the Bible and Catholic social teaching that we are all called to do God's work in this world. To love God is to love our neighbor.

This concern with justice was reinforced by our participation in the parish-based Christian Family Movement (CFM), which utilized the observe-judge-act methodology to bring Christian values to bear upon the problems of the social, economic, and political worlds in which we live. Thus, we tried to put the teachings of the specifically Christian approach to the economy embodied in Catholic social teaching into practice through local action such as lobbying the state legislature for migrant labor laws, sponsoring immigration for Dutch-Indonesians, and working in soup kitchens.

Catholics Spending and Acting Justly has grown out of my wife's and my experience in such CFM groups for over fifty years in Beaverton, Oregon; Ponce, Puerto Rico; Washington, DC; and South Bend, Indiana. The example of Christian love in action I owe to my wife, Mary Ellen Wilber, and to countless friends too numerous to mention. However, I must register my debt in particular to Ralph and Reggie Weissert, Joy and Jerry Choppin, Barbara and Lou Kuttner, and John and Marlene Olsen. I also owe much to my students at Notre Dame, both undergraduate and graduate, who challenged and taught me as I taught them.

Using This Booklet

*Christians, like all people, must be concerned
about how the concrete outcomes of their
economic activity serve human dignity; they
must assess the extent to which the structures
and practices of the economy support or
undermine their moral vision.*

—US Catholic Bishops
Economic Justice for All, #127

Y ou will likely be using *Catholics Spending and Acting Justly*
with a small group of your fellow parishioners. It will be help-
ful to designate a group facilitator to help your gatherings flow more
smoothly. This can be the same facilitator for all eight sessions, or
the role can rotate to various group members. A free leader's guide
is available for download at www.avemariapress.com. Just search
for *Catholics Spending and Acting Justly* and click on the "Extras"
tab.

Observe, Judge, Act

With the exception of the first one, the small-group sessions in this
booklet are built upon a well-tested Catholic faith sharing method —
the observe-judge-act approach. This was first developed by the late
Cardinal Joseph Cardijn, when he was a parish priest in Belgium before World War II. He inspired many Catholic social action groups
all rooted in his model of faith sharing.

After your first session when you will just be getting to know
each other, you will begin each week by reflecting together on a
scripture passage. Although your leader will have someone read this
aloud, it's a good idea to bring your own bible along if you like to
follow along.

The social inquiry part of each session utilizes the observe-judge-act approach. It works in the following way. We *observe* a situation from daily life, *judge* whether or not the situation needs to be changed, and agree to *act* in order to help bring about the desired change. Observations are most often gleaned from information obtained by consulting various sources. These observations are *events*, such as your county wanting to raise property taxes; *statistics*, such as the percentage unemployed in our county increased to 10 percent; *opinions of others*, such as five out of seven neighbors you talked with think more funds need to be spent on the local high school; or *your own experiences*, such as men get promoted ahead of women at your place of employment, even when the women are clearly more qualified.

The sources of information are important, of course. Information from several different places, with varying points of view, will usually give a better view of reality than you will glean from a single source. So, for example, read both the *New York Times* and the *Washington Times*, watch both Fox News and MSNBC. It's not enough to simply gather facts from sources with whom you tend to agree. Listen to a variety of presentations and interpretations of the event, statistic, or opinion you are observing before you begin to evaluate or judge it. While it is never possible to be completely objective about an observation, do what you can as an individual and as a group to get close.

While the observe section tries to answer the question, "What is really going on here?" the judge section uses our Christian faith to evaluate the reality observed and answer the question, "How can we make it better?" We make it better when we are able to advance human dignity.

Answering, "How can we make it better?" leads to the act section of the process. The best actions are those that grow out of your group's discussion of the observations and the judgments you reach by applying Catholic social teaching to those observations. The actions suggested are just that—suggestions. Your group will have ideas of its own, some far better suited to your situation than what we offer here.

Reference Texts

In this booklet you will find reference to a significant number of official teaching documents that belong to a rich body of work most commonly known as Catholic social teaching. The downloadable leader's guide contains a reference handout with brief descriptions of these documents, arranged by publication dates. Keep this handout with your booklet as it will be quite useful during this study. This reference list may also help direct you to deeper exploration of our Catholic faith and its social teaching tradition. An excellent sourcebook for such exploration is *A Concise Guide to Catholic Social Teaching* by Kevin E. McKenna (Ave Maria Press, 2002), from which most of these descriptions are excerpted.

Our Call to Economic Stewardship

For just as the body without a spirit is dead,
so faith without works is also dead.

—James 2:26

1. Introductions
Participants introduce themselves and say a bit about why they've joined the group.

2. Opening Prayer
Use a prayer from pages 77–79, another published prayer, or a spontaneous prayer from a group member.

3. Basic Economics and Catholic Social Teaching
Group members should read the following prior to the first meeting. Briefly review one section at a time, stopping after each for discussion, using the Questions for Conversation as a starting point.

The Crucial Role of Economic Theory

Economic theory can provide an analysis of which policies might or might not work in achieving a desired economic goal. At the core of this analysis is a model of competitive market capitalism in which it is assumed that an uncoerced person can be depended upon to act rationally in maximizing his or her individual self-interest.

Free individual choices are expected to overcome scarcity and result in people getting what they want (limited by their ability to pay) through the automatic adjustments of free exchange (buying and selling) in markets. The forces of competition ensure that the economy produces the goods that people desire and that those goods are produced in the most efficient way.

Of course, economists and casual observers alike easily recognize that this is too simple. Markets do not work so neatly. Competition is limited by large monopolistic business firms; by lack of knowledge and due concern on the part of workers, consumers, and investors; and by many other factors. For example, the model outlined above requires mobility of the factors of production, but while capital flows overseas, labor cannot follow. The result is structural domestic unemployment, at least in the short run.

Market outcomes are also distorted by the presence of "externalities" such as environmental costs. If in the act of producing automobiles, waste is dumped in a river and the people downstream have to clean up the spill, these costs are not captured in the market price of the car. This can result in a price that is too low because the cost of cleaning up the pollution is not included. More automobiles will be sold as a result of this than if the price reflected the true costs.

The resulting economic model, modified by these real-world phenomena, becomes very complicated and difficult to apply in any simple way. But let's try using three examples.

1. *What is the best way to provide reasonable housing for the poor?* Some think it is to use rent-control laws, meaning laws that fix rents below what results from the free market. However, economists argue that this is the worst way to do it. Why? Economic theory predicts that when the price of anything goes down, buyers buy more and sellers supply less. If the rent-controlled price is below what the market price would have been in its absence, then demand for housing will increase and eventually exceed the supply. All sorts of bad things can result. The excess demand can lead to corruption such as

charging under-the-table payments. The lower fixed rent will lead some potential landlords to withhold housing from the market because the return on their investments will be less. This, of course, results in a reduction in the stock of affordable housing for the poor. Some landlords will cut up their housing units into several pieces to get around the law. Others will stop maintenance because the lower fixed rent does not yield sufficient profit.

DID YOU KNOW?

According to Habitat for Humanity, a year's rent costs about 70 percent of household annual income for the 14.8 million US households that make $10,000 or less per year.

Most economists argue that if you do not like market results, you need to interfere in a way that does not make matters worse. So, for example, in the case of housing for the poor, a better way is to subsidize the poor with vouchers so that they can rent in the open market. The only requirement of the landlord is to meet local building codes. Giving renters more to spend encourages landlords to supply additional housing.

2. *The regulation of international trade.* In order for us to be able to sell our products overseas, we have to buy roughly an equal amount from abroad. To get the dollars to buy our products, other nations have to sell their products to us. So a simple protectionist policy of trying to reduce imports will make it more difficult for us to sell our export products. In addition, of course, other countries will retaliate and raise tariffs and quotas on our exports. It becomes a lose-lose game.

An additional problem is that there can be great dislocation costs as jobs are lost in an industry being hurt by imports. Replacement jobs in export industries are not always created at the same rate. Thus, trade adjustment funds need to be made available to retrain workers and to aid businesses in changing their type of production.

A close look at the comparative labor and environmental conditions of production in the trading countries is also required. These matters need to be taken into account in negotiations over reductions in trade barriers.

DID YOU KNOW?

Forrester Research Inc. predicts US employers will have moved 3.4 million white-collar jobs and $136 billion in wages overseas by 2015. A University of California at Berkeley report exceeds those projections, claiming that 14 million jobs are at risk of being sent offshore.

3. *The issue of energy conservation.* Let's examine what happens when economic theory and the real economy meet. Generally, economists argue that if you want people to economize on something, then you need to figure out how to raise its price. For example, it is not enough to exhort people to turn down their heat to conserve energy. They will be more likely to do so if heating costs are raised via an excise or sales tax. If we want to discourage people from driving cars that get poor gas mileage, the best way is to make it more expensive by raising the tax on gasoline. Over time, if prices have gone up enough, people will turn down their heat and buy smaller cars. Manufacturers will produce more efficient furnaces and automobile engines that get better mileage. If the gasoline tax is used to subsidize public transit, there will likely be the added benefit of more people parking their cars and taking the bus or subway.

These examples barely touch the complexity of studying economics, and great care must be taken not to misuse these insights by ignoring the real-world qualifications that are always present. For example, while raising the tax on gasoline may eventually discourage the purchase of gas-guzzling behemoths, there are real and often painful effects from the implementation of that policy on those who can least afford such an increase now.

In addition, one must be careful about accepting the values embedded in economic theory. The promotion of self-interest and individual liberty as the highest goals, the focus on consumerism, and neglect of disparities in income distribution, can and ought to be called into question. For example, Christian thought and biblical tradition characterize self-interest to the neglect of the common good as a central aspect of *fallen* human nature, which as Christian believers we strive to overcome with prayer, good works, and the cultivation of virtue.

This quick look at economic theory will be supplemented with examination of actual economic events in the real economy during the remaining sessions of this small-group study. You will then have the opportunity to assess what you observe about the economy in light of your Catholic faith.

Questions for Conversation

When faced with everyday spending choices—such as where to buy groceries, whether or not to take advantage of a sale on clothing, or how much time you are willing to spend making money—on what values do you base your decisions?

What economic decisions most concern you right now? How do these affect you as an individual or your family? What effect do you think your economic decisions have on the common good as you understand it?

Justice in the Biblical Tradition

> *But be doers of the word, and not merely*
> *hearers who deceive themselves.*
> **—James 1:22**

The Old Testament prophets call for social justice and condemn excessive and irresponsible wealth. For them and throughout the biblical tradition, justice is measured by a society's treatment of the powerless—most often identified as the widow, the orphan, the poor, and the stranger (non-Israelite) in the land. The prophets continually call both leaders and the people back to justice for the powerless. They direct scathing attacks at the rich and powerful who "sell the righteous for silver, and the needy for a pair of sandals—they who trample the head of the poor into the dust of the earth, and push the afflicted out of the way" (Amos 2:6–7).

Isaiah pronounces God's judgment on those "who have devoured the vineyard; rested the spoil of the poor in your houses" (3:14). Jeremiah condemns the man "who builds his house on wrong, his terraces on injustice." On the other hand, he praises King Josiah: "He judged the cause of the poor and needy; then it was well [with him]." Jeremiah then adds this startling statement: "'Is not this to know me?' says the Lord" (22:16). For the prophets, doing justice is equated with knowledge of the Lord and constitutive of true belief. Conversely, the pursuit of unfettered self-interest is seen as a stumbling block to knowing and serving God.

In the New Testament, Jesus follows closely in the tradition of the prophets, taking the side of those who are powerless or on the margin of his society. He stands up for tax collectors (Luke 15:12), the widow (Luke 7:11–17; Mark 12:41–44), the Samaritan (Luke 17:11–19), the sinful woman (Luke 7:36–50), and children (Mark 10:13–16). Jesus' description of the final judgment in Matthew's gospel is haunting with its powerful message of what is required for salvation. The most striking part of his warning is directed to those who have neglected others in need.

> "Lord, when was it that we saw you hungry or thirsty or a stranger or naked or sick or in prison, and did not take care of you?" Then he will answer them, "Truly I tell you, just as you did not do it to one of the least of these, you did not do it to me." And these will go away into eternal punishment, but the righteous into eternal life.
>
> **—Matthew 25:44–46**

Questions for Conversation

What comes to mind when you hear that the measure of a just society is its treatment of the powerless? Consider for a moment your city, parish, or household as a society. How just are you by standards of the biblical witness?

The Catholic Tradition

Catholic social teaching is rooted in a commitment to certain fundamental values derived from the biblical witness: the right to human dignity, the need for human freedom and participation, the importance of community, and the nature of the common good. These values are drawn from the belief that each person is called to be a partner with God, participating in the redemption of the world and the furthering of the Kingdom. This requires social and human development where the religious and temporal aspects of life are not separated and opposed to each other. As a result of these fundamental values, two principles permeate Catholic social teaching.

1. Special concern for the poor and powerless, which leads to a criticism of political and economic structures that oppress them.

2. Protection of certain human rights against both the collectivist tendencies of the state and the neglect of the free market.

Beginning in 1891 with Pope Leo XIII's encyclical, *Rerum Novarum* (On Capital and Labor), the Church has asserted that both state socialism and free market capitalism violate these principles. State socialism denies the right of private property, excites the envy of the poor against the rich leading to class struggle instead of cooperation, and violates the proper order of society because the state usurps the role of individuals and social groups (*Rerum Novarum*, #7–8; *Centesimus Annus* [The Hundredth Year], #13–14).

Free market capitalism denies the concept of the common good and the "social and public character of the right of property" (*Quadragesimo Anno* [On Reconstructing the Social Order], #46), including the principle of the universal destination of the earth's goods (*Rerum Novarum*, #14; *Centesimus Annus,* #6). This principal says, in brief, that the bounty of the earth has been given by God to all people equally—without exception and without preference. Free market capitalism also violates human dignity by treating labor merely as a commodity to be bought and sold in the marketplace (*Rerum Novarum*, #31; *Quadragesimo Anno*, #83; *Centesimus Annus,* #33–35). Pope John Paul II summarizes the thrust of Catholic social teaching on these matters.

> The individual today is often suffocated between two poles represented by the state and the marketplace. At times it seems as though he exists only as a producer and consumer of goods, or as an object of state administration. People lose sight of the fact that life in society has neither the market nor the state as its final purpose, since life itself has a unique value, which the state and the market must serve.
>
> —**Pope John Paul II**
> *Centesimus Annus*, #49

The concept of the common good in Catholic teaching emphasizes both the dignity of the human person and the essentially social nature of that dignity. Civil and political liberties on the one hand and social and economic needs on the other are essential components of the common good. The common good is not the aggregate or sum of the welfare of all individuals. Rather, it is a set of social conditions necessary for the realization of human dignity. These conditions transcend the arena of private exchange and contract and are essentially relational. To exist they must exist as shared. Catholic social teaching goes on to say that in pursuing the common good, special concern must be given to the economy's impact on the poor and powerless because they are particularly vulnerable (*Centesimus Annus*, #11).

> The economic sphere is neither ethically neutral, nor inherently inhuman and opposed to society. It is part and parcel of human activity and precisely because it is human, it must be structured and governed in an ethical manner.
>
> **—Pope Benedict XVI**
> *Caritas in Veritate, #36*

The Church teaches that the level of unemployment, the degree of poverty, the quantity of environmental destruction, and other harmful economic outcomes should not be left solely to the dictates of the market. Emphasis on the common good means that the community has an obligation to ensure the right of employment to all persons (*Centesimus Annus*, #15), to help the disadvantaged overcome their poverty (*Centesimus Annus*, #19, #40), and to safeguard the environment (*Centesimus Annus*, #37) for the sake of the human community it sustains.

Although Catholic social teaching defends the right to private ownership of productive property (*Rerum Novarum*, #10, #15, #36), the common good sometimes demands that this right be limited by the community through state regulation, taxation, and even—under exceptional circumstances—public ownership (*Populorum Progressio* [The Development of Peoples], #23). Pope John Paul II points out that in *Rerum Novarum* Leo XIII "is well aware that private property is not an absolute value, nor does he fail to proclaim the necessary complementary principles, such as the universal destination of the earth's goods" (*Centesimus Annus,* #6, #30). The attainment and safeguarding of human rights sometimes requires the overriding of market outcomes. Therefore, Catholic social teaching insists that "government has a moral function: protecting human rights and securing basic justice for all members of the common-wealth" (*Pacem in Terris, #60–62*).

Pope John Paul II says society and the state have the duty of "defending the basic rights of workers," defending those "collective and qualitative needs which cannot be satisfied by market mechanisms," and "overseeing and directing the exercise of human rights in the economic sector" (*Centesimus Annus, #40, #48*).

As Catholics, we understand society as a dense network of relationships among individuals, families, churches, neighborhood associations, business firms, labor unions, and different levels of government. Thus, every level of society has a role to play in ensuring basic human rights and the common good. This is expressed in the principle of subsidiarity articulated by Pope Pius XI in *Quadragesimo Anno* in 1931.

The principle of subsidiarity provides for a pluralism of social actors. Each—from the individual person to the federal government—has obligations. Higher levels should not usurp the authority of lower levels except when necessary. However, the principle works both ways. When individuals, families, or local communities are unable to solve problems that undermine the common good, the state governments are obligated to intervene, and if their resources and abilities are inadequate, then the federal government assumes the responsibility. This principle also extends into the international economy. As Pope John Paul II says, "This increasing internationalization of the economy ought to be accompanied by effective international agencies which will oversee and direct the economy to the common good, something that an individual state, even if it were the most powerful on earth, would not be in a position to do" (*Centesimus Annus, #58*).

The right to private property and the principle of subsidiarity limit the role of the state while the principle of solidarity (*Centesimus Annus, #15*) requires that society and the state intervene in markets to protect human rights, particularly of the poorest. The thrust of Catholic social teaching, therefore, has been to repudiate both state socialism and free market capitalism. What economic system does it endorse? Explicitly, none. As Pope John Paul II says, "The Church has no models to present" of the best economic system (*Centesimus Annus,* #43). That is for history to decide in each individual case. However, Catholic teaching implies a preference for a regulated market economy that protects the poor, defends human rights, allows all to participate in social groups such as trade unions, and controls market failures such as environmental pollution and persistently high unemployment. The degree of regulation is not a matter of principle but rather a case of prudential judgment in particular cases.

The US Catholic Bishops summarized this tradition of Catholic social teaching and applied it to the US economy in their 1986 pastoral letter *Economic Justice for All*:

> Catholic social teaching has traditionally rejected [these] ideological extremes because they are likely to produce results contrary to human dignity and economic justice. Starting with the assumption that the economy has been created by human beings and can be changed by them, the Church works for improvement in a variety of economic and political contexts; but it is not the Church's role to create or promote a specific new economic system. Rather, the Church must encourage all reforms that hold out hope of transforming our economic arrangements into a fuller systemic realization of the Christian moral vision. The Church must also stand ready to challenge practices and institutions that impede or carry us farther away from realizing this vision.
>
> **—US Catholic Bishops**
> *Economic Justice for All*, #128–129

Questions for Conversation

Which kind of economic system do you personally tend to favor? What in your experience has led you to this preference?

Is what you are now learning causing you to rethink your opinion about economic theory and/or practice? If so, in what ways? If not, why not?

Assessing Economic Choices in Light of Catholic Teaching

The US Catholic Bishops go on to say, "Decisions must be judged in light of what they do *for* the poor, what they do *to* the poor and what they enable the poor to do *for themselves*. The fundamental moral criterion for all economic decisions, policies, and institutions is this: They must be at the service of all people, especially the poor" (*Economic Justice for All*, #24). The following seven major themes form the core of Catholic social teaching over the last century and flesh out the call to evaluate every economic policy by what it does for people and to people, and how it allows people to do for themselves (participate in society).

1. **Dignity of the Human Person:** All people are sacred, made in the image and likeness of God. People do not lose dignity because of disability, poverty, age, lack of success, or race. People who are homeless or addicted are as important to God as physicians and world leaders. This emphasizes people over things, being over having.

2. **Community and the Common Good:** The human person is both sacred and social. We realize our dignity and rights in relationship with others, in community. We are one body; when one suffers, we all suffer. We are called to respect all of God's gifts of creation, to be good stewards of the earth and each other.

3. **Rights and Responsibilities:** People have a fundamental right to life, food, shelter, health care, education, and employment. If this means they must immigrate to secure these rights, they are entitled to do so. All people have a right to participate in decisions that affect their lives. Corresponding to these rights

are duties and responsibilities to respect the rights of others in the wider society and to work for the common good.

4. **Option for the Poor:** The moral test of a society is how it treats its most vulnerable members. The poor have the most urgent moral claim on the conscience of the nation. We are called to look at public policy decisions in terms of how they affect the poor.

5. **Dignity of Work:** People have a right to decent and productive work, fair wages, private property, and economic initiative. The economy exists to serve people, not the other way around.

6. **Solidarity:** We are one human family. Our responsibilities to each other cross national, racial, economic, and ideological differences. We are called to work globally for justice. In the economic arena as in other areas of life, competition must be complemented with cooperation.

7. **Subsidiarity:** Catholic thought sees society as made up of a dense network of relations among individuals, families, churches, neighborhood associations, business firms, labor unions, and different levels of government. Thus, every level of society has a role to play in ensuring basic human rights and the common good.

Questions to Act On

Read the following excerpt and share with your group the two or three questions that most resonate with you. During the coming week, explore these further and write responses to at least one that you can then share with your group at the next meeting.

With what care, human kindness, and justice do I conduct myself at work? How will my economic decisions to buy, sell, invest, divest, hire, or fire serve human dignity and the common good? In what career can I best exercise my talents so as to fill the world with the Spirit of Christ? How do my economic choices contribute to the strength of my family and community, to the values of my children, to sensitivity to those in need? In this consumer society, how can I develop a healthy detachment from things and avoid the temptation to assess who I am by what I have? How do I strike a balance between labor and leisure that enlarges my capacity for friendships, for family life, for community? What government policies should I support to attain the well-being of all, especially the poor and vulnerable?

—**US Catholic Bishops**
Economic Justice for All, Pastoral Message, #23

4. Looking Ahead

Have a group member read aloud next week's observes on page 19. Decide together who will do which of these (you need not do them all) and share ideas about how to go about the observes. Remember to decide together whether you will read the other material ahead of the next meeting or wait until you are gathered.

5. Closing Prayer

Close with one of the prayers found on pages 80–82, another published prayer, or a spontaneous prayer by a member of the group.

The Dignity of the Human Person

1. Opening Prayer

Use a prayer from pages 77–79, another published prayer, or a spontaneous prayer from a group member.

2. Report on Previous Meeting's Action

Spend a few minutes sharing responses to the questions posed by the excerpt from Economic Justice for All *at the end of last week's meeting.*

3. Scriptural Reflection: *Psalm 139:1–6, 13–18*

A member of the group reads the passage aloud. All then reflect in silence or in conversation.

Do you truly believe that you are good because God has made you? What about your life helps or hinders this belief? How does this fundamental tenet of our faith influence the way you live each day?

4. Social Inquiry: Observe, Judge, Act

> The human person is the clearest reflection of God's presence in the world; all of the Church's work in pursuit of both justice and peace is designed to protect and promote the dignity of every person.
>
> **—US Catholic Bishops**
> *The Challenge of Peace, #15*

All people are sacred, and our Christian faith requires us to value people over things, being over having. Because of these fundamental

DID YOU KNOW?

The wealthiest 20 percent of the world's people account for over 75 percent of total private consumption while the poorest 20 percent account for only about 1.5 percent.

values, we have a number of reasons to be concerned with the way our economy works, particularly the emphasis on consumption. First, while consumption spending helps people by creating jobs, excessive consumption by some individuals and nations while at the same time other individuals and nations suffer from want is morally unacceptable. Pope Paul VI affirms this teaching in *Populorum Progressio*, #49:

> [T]he superfluous wealth of rich countries should be placed at the service of poor nations. . . . Otherwise their continued greed will certainly call down upon them the judgment of God and the wrath of the poor.

In addition to avoiding over-consumption while others go without basic necessities, consumers have an obligation to avoid consuming products made under inhuman conditions.

Second, excessive production and consumption that threaten the earth's environment are also morally unacceptable.

> In his desire to have and to enjoy rather than to be and to grow, [man] consumes the resources of the earth and his own life in an excessive and distorted way.
>
> **—Pope John Paul II**
> *Centesimus Annus*, #37

Third, treating consumption as the primary goal of economic life—that is, focusing on *having* instead of *being*—fails to respect the human dignity of consumers themselves. In contrast to the communitarian basis of Catholic social teaching, our economy is rooted in an individualist conception of society. Society is seen as a collection of individuals who have chosen to associate because it is mutually beneficial. Individual liberty is the highest good, and, if individuals are left free to pursue their self-interest, the result will be the maximum material welfare. People are seen as hedonists who want to maximize pleasure and minimize pain. It is assumed that pleasure comes primarily from the consumption of goods and services, and that pain comes primarily from work and from parting with income. Thus, given resource constraints, the goal of the economy should be to maximize the production of goods and services that people want and can demand with their dollar votes. In short, more is always better.

Catholic social teaching, however, condemns this materialist view of human welfare.

> Increased possession is not the ultimate goal of nations or of individuals. All growth is ambivalent. It is essential if man is to develop as a man, but in a way it imprisons man if he considers it the supreme good, and it restricts his vision. Then we see hearts harden and minds close, and men no longer gather together in friendship but out of self-interest, which soon leads to oppositions and disunity. The exclusive pursuit of possessions thus becomes an obstacle to individual fulfillment and to man's true greatness.

> — **Pope Paul VI**
> *Populorum Progressio*, #19

Unfortunately, in modern industrial economies, whether advanced or developing, it is perfectly rational for people to accept a philosophy of consumerism.

People have little opportunity to choose meaningful work because the nature of employment is determined by competitive pressures. The demand for labor

DID YOU KNOW?

The richest fifth of the world's population consumes 58 percent of total energy output, while the poorest fifth consumes less than 4 percent.

mobility disrupts the sense of community found in traditional settings. And the enjoyment of nature is attenuated by urbanization and the degradation of nature resulting from industrial and consumption practices. Thus, the only thing left under the individual's control is consumption and consumption can substitute, however inadequately, for the loss of meaningful work, community, and a decent environment. With enough income, people can buy bottled water, place their children in private schools, buy a mountain cabin, and obtain the education necessary to get a more interesting job. Of course, for the vast majority of people, this is just a dream.

Our faith calls us to measure this economy not only by what it produces, but also by how it touches human life and whether it protects or undermines the dignity of the human person. Economic decisions have human consequences and moral content; they help or hurt people, strengthen or weaken family life, advance or diminish the quality of justice in our land.

—US Catholic Bishops
Economic Justice for All, Pastoral Message, #1

DID YOU KNOW?

Americans spend $8 billion each year on cosmetics, while it would take only $14 billion to provide universal access to basic education.

Paul Wachtel says in *The Poverty of Affluence* (1983) that growth in the economy no longer brings a sense of greater well-being, and the reason why the pleasures our new possessions bring melt into thin air is that at the level of affluence of the American middle class what really matters is not one's possessions but one's psychological well-being. We have constructed a culture in which the contribution of material goods to life satisfaction has reached a point of diminishing returns. He adds that the creative and rewarding use of leisure should be at least as central a concern in the economy as the need for sustaining meaningful work.

It is not wrong to want to live better; what is wrong is a style of life which is presumed to be better when it is directed toward having rather than being, and which wants to have more, not in order to be more but in order to spend life in enjoyment as an end in itself.

—Pope John Paul II
Centesimus Annus, #36

Observe

1. There are five people aboard a small airplane in a violent storm. The pilot has died from a heart attack, and no one knows how to fly the plane, which is losing altitude quickly. The five people aboard are (1) a young pregnant woman with an incurable disease; (2) a wealthy philanthropist; (3) an illegal immigrant; (4) a cardinal archbishop beloved by the people of his diocese; and (5) a famous movie star. There are only three parachutes.

2. Who in your community suffers from not having their human dignity respected? Minorities? Day laborers? Illegal immigrants? The homeless? Why does this appear to be the case?

3. Have you ever felt your human dignity was not respected? What were the circumstances?

4. Do new goods make you happy? How so? For how long? Do some more than others?

Judge

1. In observe #1 there are three parachutes, so two people will perish when the plane crashes. To which three persons would you give parachutes and what are the reasons for your choices?

What do your choices tell you about your values? How do these values match up with your Catholic beliefs?

2. What criteria underlie Catholic teaching about the dignity of the human person? How does this differ from how our society values the person?

3. In your own life—personal and economic—how can you live out the principle of honoring every person's human dignity?

4. How can you keep your consumption from detracting from your life as a Christian?

Act

1. Treat all people you encounter this week as a "clear reflection of God's presence in the world."

2. Study your family's consumption pattern and decide if you are putting things before persons. If so make a change.

3. Volunteer with a community organization that helps people who are poor, homeless, hungry, disabled, or otherwise marginalized.

DID YOU KNOW?

In Europe, the equivalent of US$11 billion is spent each year on ice cream. For $19 billion, the global community could provide universal access to clean water and sanitation.

4. Choose two days during the week to abstain from meat and fish. The early Church did so on Wednesdays and Fridays. Offer this sacrifice in union with all those that are hungry in the world and donate the money you save to your local soup kitchen to help feed the poor.

5. Monitor your household use of electricity and gas. Set goals to reduce overall consumption that will in turn save money. Donate the money saved to help those in need keep their homes heated during the winter months. Your local utility company will most likely have a fund set up for this purpose.

6. Thinking of a family vacation for the upcoming year? Rather than visiting an expensive resort, embrace the beauty of God's creation by visiting a national or state park. The money you save can be used to help children appreciate nature. www.childrenandnature.org/

7. Monitor how much your household spends on cigarettes, alcohol, cosmetics, perfumes, candy, and ice cream. Cut this expenditure in half and donate your savings to those in need.

5. Looking Ahead
Have a group member read aloud next week's observes on page 28. Decide together who will do which of these (you need not do them all) and share ideas about how to go about the observes.

6. Closing Prayer
Close with one of the prayers found on pages 80–82, another published prayer, or a spontaneous prayer by a member of the group.

Community and the Common Good

1. Opening Prayer

Use a prayer from pages 77–79, another published prayer, or a spontaneous prayer from a group member.

2. Report on Previous Meeting's Action

Spend a few minutes reporting on the progress of your acts from the last meeting.

3. Scriptural Reflection: *1 Corinthians 12:12–26* and *Acts 4:32–35*

A member of the group reads the passage aloud. All then reflect in silence or in conversation.

Which parts of these readings most resonate with what you have been learning about Catholic social teaching? What challenge do these passages hold for you today? How will you try to meet that challenge?

4. Social Inquiry: Observe, Judge, Act

Possibly the most important difference between the philosophy that animates our economy and Catholic social teaching is that the former is based on an individualist conception of society and the latter on a communitarian vision.

Historically, modern economics, usually dated from the 1776 publication of Adam Smith's *The Wealth of Nations,* developed within an individualist and utilitarian philosophy. The core of this economic philosophy is the model of competitive market capitalism.

DID YOU KNOW?

Individualist and consumerist mentalities are formed early in life. The average child in the United States is in school for 900 hours a year. In that same time period, that child will watch 1,500 hours of television and view 20,000 thirty-second commercials.

As discussed in the first session, this philosophy asserts that an uncoerced person can be depended upon to act rationally in maximizing his or her individual self-interest. More importantly, it is thought that an automatic, self-regulating mechanism to manage economic affairs is possible if it is built on this basic human nature. Free individual choices are expected to overcome scarcity and result in the common good through the automatic adjustments of free exchange in markets. The forces of competition ensure that the economy produces those goods that people desire and that maximum output is produced at a given cost or cost is minimized for a given output.

The fact that most economies are characterized by widespread poverty, unemployment, and low wages poses a problem to economists. The claim to overcome scarcity seems to ring hollow. They explain it in two ways. First, there are those countries that restrict the free operation of markets. If they would remove the restrictions to the free play of self-interest, much of the poverty would be eliminated by the resulting economic growth. Second, in those countries that have free market systems, continuing poverty is explained as being the result of the stinginess of the natural environment (poor soils, lack of natural resources, etc.) and the improvidence of human nature.

Only educating people to overcome their natural lethargy can reduce poverty, caused by the improvidence of human nature. Changing economic structures will not make any difference, except to the extent that existing social institutions misdirect the decision-making ability of rational individuals. The individualist/rationalist tradition of the West, with its emphasis on achievement and attribution of responsibility to individuals, lends credence to this view. Hard work, thrift, and prudence always have been seen as the keys to success. Failure has been attributed to a lack of these values. Systemic causes of the failure to ensure material well-being to all have been neglected; instead, blame is placed on personal characteristics.

In contrast, the concept of the common good in Catholic social teaching is rooted in a communitarian vision of society. Because of this, it emphasizes both the dignity of the human person and the essentially social nature of that dignity. Both civil and political liberties on the one hand and social and economic needs on the other are essential components of the common good.

Gaudium et Spes defines the common good as "the sum of those conditions of social life which allow social groups and their individual members relatively thorough and ready access to their own fulfillment" (#26). As we saw in the first session, the common good is not the aggregate of the welfare of all individuals. Rather, it is a set of social conditions necessary for the realization of human dignity. For example, "such goods as political self-determination, participation in the economic productivity of an industrialized society, and enjoyment

DID YOU KNOW?

22,000 children die each day worldwide—that's fifteen every minute—due to poverty, hunger, and easily preventable diseases and illnesses. Despite the scale of this ongoing catastrophe, it rarely manages to achieve, much less sustain, headline news coverage.

of one's cultural heritage can be obtained by an individual only through participation in the public life of society" (David Hollenbach, *Claims in Conflict*, p. 147). Claims on these goods are social rights such as freedom to assemble, work, and adequate health care.

To desire the *common good* and strive towards it *is a requirement of justice and charity.* To take a stand for the common good is on the one hand to be solicitous for, and on the other hand to avail oneself of, that complex of institutions that give structure to the life of society — juridically, civilly, politically and culturally, making it the *polis*, or "city." The more we strive to secure a common good corresponding to the real needs of our neighbors, the more effectively we love them. Every Christian is called to practice this charity, in a manner corresponding to his vocation and according to the degree of influence he wields in the polis. This is the institutional path — we might also call it the political path — of charity, no less excellent and effective than the kind of charity that encounters the neighbor directly, outside the institutional mediation of the polis.

— **Pope Benedict XVI**
Caritas in Veritate, #7

Emphasis on the common good means that the community has an obligation to guarantee the right of employment, to help the disadvantaged overcome their poverty, and to safeguard the environment. Catholic teaching defends the right to private ownership of productive property (*Rerum Novarum*, #10, #15, #36), but the common good sometimes demands that this right be limited by the community through state regulation, taxation, and even public ownership (*Populorum Progressio*, #23). Thus, the attainment and safeguarding of human rights sometimes requires the overriding of market outcomes.

Pope John XXIII summarizes the basic teaching on the role of the state as given by Pope Leo XIII in 1891:

The state, whose purpose is the realization of the common good in the temporal order, can by no means disregard the economic activities of its citizens. Indeed, it should be present to promote in a suitable manner the production of a sufficient supply of material goods . . . safeguard the rights of all citizens, but especially the weaker, such as workers, women, and children.

—Pope John XXIII
Mater et Magistra, #20–21

In addition to its purely spiritual functions, the Church, as a community, plays four distinct but interrelated roles in the economy and in society more generally.

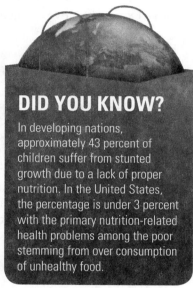

DID YOU KNOW?

In developing nations, approximately 43 percent of children suffer from stunted growth due to a lack of proper nutrition. In the United States, the percentage is under 3 percent with the primary nutrition-related health problems among the poor stemming from over consumption of unhealthy food.

1. Standing for certain fundamental values in the public arena: truth, justice, solidarity, human rights, and peace. The Church proclaims that these values are more important than economic efficiency, political realism, or technical virtuosity.

2. Adding its distinctive analysis and prescriptions to the process of policy-formation in our pluralistic society. The Church speaks as a body of citizens with a special view of what economic and social policy ought to be. It does this in areas as diverse as tax policy (to plead for equity therein), housing policy, welfare policy for the poor, and employment programs.

3. Engaging in local problem-solving actions. For centuries the Church has engaged in works that institutionalize the corporal works of mercy—feeding the hungry, healing the sick, consoling prisoners, and educating the ignorant.

4. Practicing solidarity with those who are persecuted or victimized in some fashion by natural or humanly caused disasters. Early Christian churches in scattered points of the Roman Empire took up collections to aid the impoverished local church in Jerusalem. Similarly, in our day, the Church operates relief and

development programs, such as Catholic Relief Services, to assist groups in need throughout the world.

All of these so-called secular roles flow from the Church as a community of believers bound together by Christ's command to love God and to love our neighbor as ourselves.

Observe

1. Ask several neighbors or coworkers whom they consider to be part of their community. Does it include people of other races or economic standing, immigrants (legal and undocumented), people of other religious backgrounds or levels of education, and people they dislike?

When an alien resides with you in your land, you shall not oppress the alien. The alien who resides with you shall be to you as the citizen among you; you shall love the alien as yourself, for you were once aliens in the land of Egypt: I am the Lord your God.

—Leviticus 19:33–34

---

2. Ask several Christians outside this small group what they think marks their church community as Christian. In the early Church it was said "they knew we were Christians by our love." Is that the key feature today?

3. Ask several Catholics you know what they think about the four secular roles of the Church listed above.

4. Is your parish a community in the sense envisioned in Catholic social teaching? Explain with examples.

5. Make a list of local church activities that serve the community.

Judge

1. What priority in time, energy, or commitment of resources should serving your neighbor have in your life? How can you as individuals and families make this more central? What more should your parish be doing? What are the risks in being a good neighbor?

2. If in your observations there were people left out of the community, is there anything that should be done for them?

3. Can you in good conscience ignore the political process as it involves serving others, particularly the poor and disadvantaged? What are you or might you be doing to stay involved in political activities on behalf of those in need?

4. Is a vibrant community important for people's human dignity?

Love—*caritas*—is an extraordinary force that leads people to opt for courageous and generous engagement in the field of justice and peace.

—Pope Benedict XVI
Caritas in Veritate, #1

Act

1. Prepare a list of what you consider to be important goals and ideals in your life, for your family, and for the broader community. Examine your stance on government programs versus private charities that serve the poor. Where do you stand on consumerism versus living a simple life? Finally, set down your actual budget of expenditures. How does what you spend match what you profess? How not? Are there ways you can change? This exercise is for your own benefit and does not have to be shared with the group.

2. Talk with your parish priest, other pastoral staff members, and parish pastoral council about what can be done to make the parish a better community.

3. Investigate to see in what ways you can become a more active member of your parish community and/or of the broader community and then act upon that possibility.

4. Support local businesses by shopping at your local markets and small bookstores, eating at local restaurants, and supporting local cultural centers (museums, theatres, coffee houses, etc.).

5. Take part in volunteer opportunities for Catholic religious education. Help with the RCIA, teach catechism, or start a Bible study.

6. Get to know your neighbors by inviting them for dinner or a movie night. Or organize a neighborhood gathering with the express purpose of not only getting to know each other, but also identifying how you might help each other out.

5. Looking Ahead
Have a group member read aloud next week's observes on pages 35–36. Decide together who will do which of these (you need not do them all) and share ideas about how to go about the observes.

6. Closing Prayer
Close with one of the prayers found on pages 80–82, another published prayer, or a spontaneous prayer by a member of the group.

SESSION 4

Rights and Responsibilities

1. Opening Prayer
Use a prayer from pages 77–79, another published prayer, or a spontaneous prayer from a group member.

2. Report on Previous Meeting's Action
Spend a few minutes reporting on the progress of your acts from the last meeting.

3. Scriptural Reflection: *Tobit 4:14–19* and *Luke 16:19–31*
A member of the group reads the passages aloud. All then reflect in silence or in conversation.

Consider the teaching from Tobit and what you know of Catholic social teaching. What are Lazarus's rights and the rich man's responsibilities? What are some of your social rights and responsibilities as part of local and global communities?

4. Social Inquiry: Observe, Judge, Act

As we explored earlier, the Church tells us that individuals have rights to what they need to live with dignity. These rights are derived from a person's membership in a community, not simply from his or her nature as an isolated individual. As the US Bishops say in their pastoral letter on the economy: "The virtues of good citizenship require a lively sense of participation in the commonwealth and of having obligations as well as rights within it" (*Economic Justice for All*, #296).

In his encyclical *Pacem in Terris*, Pope John XXIII sets out in detail a full range of human rights that can only be realized and protected in solidarity with others. These rights include the civil and political rights to freedom of speech, worship, and assembly. He also includes a number of economic rights concerning human welfare. First among these are the rights to life, food, clothing, shelter, rest, medical care, and basic education. In order to ensure these rights everyone has the right to earn a living. Everyone also has a right to security in the event of illness, unemployment, or old age. The right to participate in the community requires the right of employment, as well as the right to healthful working conditions, wages, and other benefits sufficient to support families at a level in keeping with human dignity.

Many people today would claim that they owe nothing to anyone, except to themselves. They are concerned only with their rights, and they often have great difficulty in taking responsibility for their own and other people's integral development. Hence it is important to call for a renewed reflection on how *rights presuppose duties, if they are not to become mere license*. . . . A link has often been noted between claims to a "right to excess," and even to transgression and vice, within affluent societies, and the lack of food, drinkable water, basic instruction and elementary health care in areas of the underdeveloped world and on the outskirts of large metropolitan centers. The link consists in this: individual rights, when detached from a framework of duties which grants them their full meaning, can run wild, leading to an escalation of demands which is effectively unlimited and indiscriminate.

—Pope Benedict XVI
Caritas in Veritate, #43

The Church places a two-fold obligation upon individual Christians to help the community to attain and safeguard these social and economic rights. First, individuals are called upon to support efforts, through the state and other appropriate institutions, to aid the poor and disadvantaged. This includes the obligation to support, with tax monies and votes, appropriate legislation proposed by elected officials—economic policies to attain full employment, income support programs to counter poverty, health care systems, and so on. The Gospel message also obligates individual Christians to draw upon their surplus to meet the needs of the poor through support of voluntary charities and other private groups dedicated to help the poor.

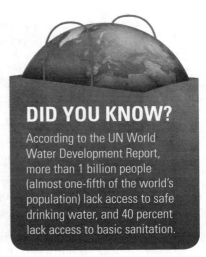

DID YOU KNOW?

According to the UN World Water Development Report, more than 1 billion people (almost one-fifth of the world's population) lack access to safe drinking water, and 40 percent lack access to basic sanitation.

In *Economic Justice for All*, the US Bishops remind us that government plays a crucial role in safeguarding social and economic rights, especially on behalf of those who are poor or disadvantaged.

> Government should assume a positive role in generating employment and establishing fair labor practices, in guaranteeing the provision and maintenance of the economy's infrastructure, such as roads, bridges, harbors, public means of communication, and transport. It should regulate trade and commerce in the interest of fairness. Government may levy the taxes necessary to meet these responsibilities, and citizens have a moral obligation to pay those taxes. The way society responds to the needs of the poor through its public policies is the litmus test of its justice or injustice. The political debate about these policies is the indispensable forum for dealing with the

conflicts and trade-offs that will always be present in the
pursuit of a more just economy.

—**US Catholic Bishops**
Economic Justice for All, #123

A just system of taxation is one that is based on ability to pay and
preserves incentives to save and invest. Pope Leo XIII warns against
confiscatory taxes that destroy property rights and incentives. Pope
Pius XI notes that this warning does not preclude progressive taxation that bears heavily on the wealthy. Sharing the common burdens
in accord with ability to pay actually protects property against social
disorder. Pope Pius XII emphasizes the need to preserve economic
incentives. Pope John XXIII argues, "As regards taxation, assess-
ment according to ability to pay is fundamental to a just and equi-
table tax system" (*Mater et Magistra*, #132).

Thus, two considerations must
be balanced in developing a just
tax system. On the one hand, the
factors of equality of sacrifice and
ability to pay dictate progressive income taxes. On the other, retaining
profit incentives and stimulating
savings and investment is necessary for economic growth and job
creation. In addition, all taxes have
social implications. A general sales
tax is regressive in its incidence: as
household income increases, the
percentage of that income spent on
taxed consumer items goes down

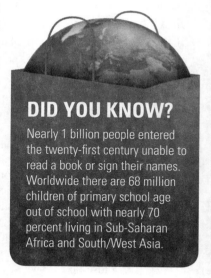

DID YOU KNOW?

Nearly 1 billion people entered
the twenty-first century unable to
read a book or sign their names.
Worldwide there are 68 million
children of primary school age
out of school with nearly 70
percent living in Sub-Saharan
Africa and South/West Asia.

and the amount saved goes up. The result is that the tax paid as a
percent of income is inversely related to income. For example, if
a sales tax is 4 percent on all consumption goods and services and
poor people spend 100 percent of their income on those items, then

the tax rate on their income is 4 percent. If rich people spend only 50 percent of their income on taxed consumption goods, then the tax rate on their income falls to 2 percent.

Another factor to consider is that taxes on a product or service cause the price to increase and sales to decline. Sometimes this is deliberate such as with taxes on alcohol and tobacco and sometimes it is an unintended consequence. Clearly each new tax needs to be evaluated for its impact on equity and on economic efficiency in addition to revenue generation.

The state is not the only means of protecting rights and exercising duties. We as individuals and as members of intermediate groups such as families, parishes, and civic groups also have obligations. There will be more of this in the session on subsidiarity.

Profit is useful if it serves as a means towards an end that provides a sense both of how to produce it and how to make good use of it. Once profit becomes the exclusive goal, if it is produced by improper means and without the common good as its ultimate end, it risks destroying wealth and creating poverty.

—Pope Benedict XVI
Caritas in Veritate, #21

Observe

1. Find out what the unemployment rate is in your community. Ask an unemployed person, an employed worker, and an employer for their opinion on why the rate is what it is.

2. Find out what the high school graduation rate is in your community. Ask someone in the school superintendent's office why it is that rate.

3. Find out the extent of untreated medical problems in your community. If there is a public clinic, ask someone there what they think is the extent of the problem. You might also ask your

family physician and someone in the emergency room of the
local hospital.

4.   Ask three people if they would be willing to pay higher taxes
to help meliorate the problems you may have uncovered. Ask
them why or why not.

Judge

1.   Since we are our brother's and sister's keeper, how does
that translate into our role as citizens, as parishioners, as
individuals?

2.   The fact that we are our brother's and sister's keeper doesn't
tell us how to do so. Using what you know of Catholic social
teaching, explain how you would argue for a "liberal" policy
and for a "conservative" policy to overcome unemployment,
poverty, or lack of medical care for those without adequate insurance. Do the varying perspectives hinge upon differences
in values or in different understandings of observable realities,
(i.e., whether markets work well, government is corrupt, or
there is lots or little monopoly in the economy)?

3.   How great is your obligation to help others? How great is each
person's obligation to help himself or herself?

[The] dual command of love that is at the basis of all Christian
morality is illustrated in the Gospel of Luke by the parable of
a Samaritan who interrupts his journey to come to the aid
of a dying man (Luke 10:29–37). Unlike the other wayfarers
who look on the man and pass by, the Samaritan "was
moved with compassion at the sight"; he stops, tends the
wounded man and takes him to a place of safety. In this
parable compassion is the bridge between mere seeing
and action; love is made real through effective action.

—US Catholic Bishops
Economic Justice for All, #43

Act

1. Find out your political party's position on helping those with food, housing, medical, and education needs. If you disagree with that position, contact their headquarters and tell them so.

2. Volunteer in a health clinic, a homeless shelter, a food pantry, or some similar place.

3. Contact your local community leaders about any shortfalls in help for those in need.

4. Start a program in your parish, for example, classes on money management, economic cooking, nutrition; a food pantry; a Thanksgiving dinner for those who have no place to go.

5. Contact your local *Sant' Egidio* or Catholic Worker community to find out about how you might assist them in their outreach ministries.

    www.santegidio.org

    www.catholicworker.org/communities

6. Visit your local assisted living or retirement home to spend time with the elderly. Bring some simple games and a good ear for listening! You might even learn a thing or two.

7. Donate maternity clothing, baby clothing, diapers, formula, household items, furniture, and appliances to your local crisis pregnancy center. These will greatly benefit mothers in need.

5. Looking Ahead
Have a group member read aloud next week's observes on pages 45–46. Decide together who will do which of these (you need not do them all) and share ideas about how to go about the observes.

6. Closing Prayer
Close with one of the prayers found on pages 80–82, another published prayer, or a spontaneous prayer by a member of the group.

SESSION 5

The Option for the Poor

1. Opening Prayer

*Use a prayer from pages 77–79, another published prayer, or a spontane-
ous prayer from a group member.*

2. Report on Previous Meeting's Action

*Spend a few minutes reporting on the progress of your acts from the last
meeting.*

3. Scriptural Reflection: *Proverbs 14:21, 31* **and** *Matthew
25:31–46*

*A member of the group reads the passages aloud. All then reflect in si-
lence or in conversation.*

**Reflect on what the hungry, the stranger, the naked, the sick, and the
prisoner share in common. Why do you think Jesus identifies with the
poor?**

**Reflect on the times you have served Christ without initially knowing
it. Does this impact your view of what it means to be a Christian?**

4. Social Inquiry: Observe, Judge, Act

Poverty is not an isolated problem existing solely among a small
number of anonymous people in our central cities. Nor is it limited
to a dependent underclass or to specific groups in the United States.
It is a condition experienced at some time by many people of different walks of life and in different circumstances. Many poor people
are working, but at wages insufficient to lift them out of poverty.
Others are unable to work and are therefore dependent on outside
sources of support. Still others are on the edge of poverty: although

not officially defined as poor, they are economically insecure and at risk of falling into poverty.

As the US Bishops say: "The themes of human dignity and the preferential option for the poor are at the heart of our approach; they compel us to confront the issue of poverty with a real sense of urgency" (*Economic Justice for All*, #186). Overcoming poverty is not a luxury that we can deal with when we find the time and resources. Rather, it is a moral priority of the highest order and urgency.

Poor and homeless people sleep in community shelters and in our church basements. The hungry fill soup kitchens. Unemployment gnaws at the self-respect of both middle-aged persons who have lost their jobs and the young who cannot find them. Hardworking men and women wonder if the system of enterprise that helped them yesterday might destroy their jobs and their communities tomorrow. Ethnic minorities often face racism, which may inhibit their full participation in the economic sphere. Many elderly people feel isolated once they retire. As life expectancy increases, the families of many older people struggle financially to care for them.

DID YOU KNOW?

According to the National Law Center on Homelessness and Poverty, approximately 3.5 million people, 1.35 million of them children, are likely to experience homelessness in a given year.

According to the US Census Bureau, the official poverty rate in 2009 was 14.3 percent—up from 13.2 percent in 2008. That means that 43.6 million people were in poverty, up from 39.8 million in 2008—the third consecutive annual increase. From 2008, the number of poor Americans grew by more than nine million. The number of people living in extreme poverty, that is, with incomes below half the poverty line, rose to over 17 million people. That is the highest level on record since data first became available in 1975. The poverty rate for children is far worse than for adults. Children make up about one quarter of our population, but nearly a third of Americans in poverty are children. Census statistics from 2008 further reveal that 8.2 percent of whites, 21.5 percent of Hispanics, 24.5 percent of African Americans, and 10.2 percent of Asian Americans were living below the poverty line. (For more facts about poverty in the United States, visit www.usccb.org/cchd/povertyusa/povfacts .shtml.) Although the precise determination of who lives in poverty may be questioned, some trends can still be traced, namely, poverty rates are rising, particularly for those groups who are already most vulnerable.

> As followers of Christ, we are challenged to make a fundamental "option for the poor"—to speak for the voiceless, to defend the defenseless, to assess life styles, policies, and social institutions in terms of their impact on the poor. This "option for the poor" does not mean pitting one group against another, but rather, strengthening the whole community by assisting those who are most vulnerable. As Christians, we are called to respond to the needs of all our brothers and sisters, but those with the greatest needs require the greatest response.
>
> —**US Catholic Bishops**
> *Economic Justice for All*, Pastoral Message, #16

Poverty exists both transitionally and transgenerationally. Each type has its distinct causes, and each affects individuals differently. Although there is some overlap, the solutions for eliminating poverty are particular to the kind of poverty being addressed.

Transitional poverty, usually of a more temporary duration, results when an individual or household living above the poverty line falls below it. Divorce, death of an income-earning spouse, retirement, unemployment, or illness may financially bind a previously economically stable person. While some struggle to overcome adversity without success, others in transitional poverty move out of their financial distress, either by their own efforts or with the help of others.

Transgenerational poverty, on the other hand, develops among children who, because they grow up in poverty, do not have equal access to adequate health care, proper nutrition, quality education, and many other societal benefits that those with higher incomes often take for granted. When pregnant women and young children lack necessary care, the youngsters will often suffer from lower intellectual abilities and missed days at school. Those who may receive satisfactory health benefits may still struggle in under funded schools, which cannot provide the necessary supplies, educational discipline, or individualized attention children and youth require. Without a good education, these children often follow their parents work history: they find employment at low paying jobs, if they qualify for any position at all, and often lack the necessary job skills to retain long-term positions. These inequalities clearly contribute to continuing the cycle of poverty for many American families.

DID YOU KNOW?

There are 2.2 billion children in the world, of which 1 billion live in poverty.

Those living in transgenerational poverty are not only materially poor; they also often lack the necessary education, job opportunities, and psychological and social tools to lift themselves out of their situation. Economic poverty can cause alienation from mainstream society, leading to destitution of other sorts that is often more serious than the initial financial inadequacies. The breaking of the human spirit—lack of hope for change and loss of meaning in life—which is so evident in the lives of many who are poor, is perhaps the deepest tragedy of economic poverty.

In some disadvantaged communities, an entire subeconomy has developed around the drug trade. Drug use entails an abuse of the human person since the commerce perpetuates the sins of physical violence, psychological intimidation, and personal material gain.

Further, profiting from another's addiction interferes with the call to respect the inherent God-given dignity of all persons. While the immediate effects of this subeconomy may be satisfying for those who profit from it, long-range effects likely include economic instability, a criminal record, and a fear of law-enforcement agents as well as both one's partners and adversaries in the drug trade.

Why do people risk all for this material gain? Although the answer is complicated, several factors must be noted that contribute to the perpetuation of this subeconomy. Many of these neighborhoods lack jobs that pay adequate wages, or, if the positions exist, training for them does not. Also, materialism, a sin that affects nearly all Americans, calls even the poorest of the poor to constantly strive for more possessions.

Materialism grows both from the market economy, which influences buyers, and from buyers, who influence markets. Because advertising so effectively encourages materialism, even those whose basic needs go unmet are enticed to purchase frivolous luxuries. Catholic social teaching encourages businesses to use their advertising influence to provide for the needs of people, rather than exploiting consumers for purely material

DID YOU KNOW?

Sixty-two percent of those defined as poor by the US Census Bureau have cable or satellite television while at least 80 percent of humanity lives on less than $10 a day.

gain. Individuals who cannot afford them need to consciously fight the lure of acquiring excessive goods. Of course, determining what are true necessities and what are excessive or simply luxury goods is a difficult and often contemptuous debate. Materialism, along with other causes of poverty, creates conflict for both businesses and individuals. Businesses must sell to earn profits, and they must earn profits to stay in business and support their workforces. Thus they are tempted to use advertising that plays on people's psychological vulnerabilities, for example, urging people to believe that buying a certain brand of shoes or driving a certain car is the only key to popularity and success. The result all too often is that people go into debt beyond their means and their whetted appetites crowd out their responsible decision-making with an unthinking materialism.

The responsibility for combating poverty exists not only within the nation, but at the global level as well. Globalization can exacerbate the problem of poverty. Though detrimental to both US workers and many third-world workers, some corporations still choose to move their production facilities from the United States to other nations where people will work for less money. When a living wage is not guaranteed and a respect for human dignity is not guarded, globalization allows for dehumanizing sweatshop conditions. While sometimes bolstering the economies of one or even many nations, globalization can often also result in the exploitation of workers, violating not only the workers but those who employ them as well.

> Despite some of its structural elements, which should neither be denied nor exaggerated, "globalization, *a priori*, is neither good nor bad. It will be what people make of it." We should not be its victims, but rather its protagonists, acting in the light of reason, guided by charity and truth. Blind opposition would be a mistaken and prejudiced attitude, incapable of recognizing the positive aspects of the process, with the consequent risk of missing the chance to take advantage of its many opportunities for development.
>
> **—Pope Benedict XVI**
> *Caritas in Veritate*, #42

Economic arrangements can be the source of fulfillment, of hope, and of community, or they may be the roots of frustration, isolation, and even despair. The economic sphere affects the quality of people's lives, even whether people live or die. Serious economic choices go beyond purely technical issues to fundamental questions of value and purpose. Through economic choices and activity, people learn virtue and vice, they derive meaning for their lives, and they define themselves by roles played in the economic world. We are fortunate to have the Christian religious and moral tradition as embodied in Catholic social teaching to help us in facing tough economic questions and helping us determine in which direction we should head.

Sustaining a common culture and commitment to moral values is essential if the economy is to serve all people more fairly. Many Americans feel themselves in the grip of economic demands and cultural pressures that go far beyond the individual's, or even the family's, capacity to cope. Decision-making within corporations too often focuses only on the profit of the company, often to the detriment of workers or the environment. Government policies, which affect the quality of life of nearly every American, must be determined with the common good in mind, but too often are driven by the contributions of lobbyists for special interest groups.

However, this vision of the common good is not easily achieved. In combating poverty, we are tempted to find solutions only in terms of economics and policy change. Too often, we see poverty as a pervasive systemic problem about which we can personally do little or nothing. Faced with this, the Church proclaims that individuals, as sacred and social beings, must do what is within their power to eliminate poverty. Neglecting this personal responsibility is contrary to the Body of Christ and the Gospels.

Observe

1. Visit the US Catholic Bishop's website on poverty in America at www.usccb.org/cchd/povertyusa/index.htm where you will find a great deal of information on poverty in the United States. See if you find information that you didn't know and surprises you. Share your findings with the group.

2. Try to find out who are the poor in your parish, in your neighborhood, your town. What is being done to help them by private groups and through public programs?

3. Find out what programs for the poor are sponsored by your parish and what ones could be.

4. Is there a need for clothing in your community? What do you do with clothing you no longer wear?

5. If you became homeless, what would you most miss about your home? Think about how this might inform your action on behalf of justice for the homeless.

6. If you know of someone with serious illness, describe the effects of that illness on his or her family.

7. Read and reflect on the following true story from Michael Kirwan in *The Catholic Worker* and come prepared to discuss it at your next session. Ask yourself if you have experienced an incident where a kind person helped you but didn't respect you and how that made you feel.

> In the winter of 1978, a young man in Washington, DC, was coming home from work on a cold night when he passed a beggar who asked for a dollar to buy food. He ignored the beggar because he assumed the money would be wasted on alcohol instead of food. But after getting home his conscience began to bother him and he made a bowl of soup. He brought it to the beggar and sat it down without saying a word. From then on he did this every night and soon attracted several more beggars. So he cooked even more soup. One night he brought a whole gallon of hot split-pea soup, set it down and turned to go. One of the beggars grabbed the jar of soup and broke it over the young man's head. He was shocked and asked: "Why did you do that?" The beggar replied: "You are doing nothing more than bringing food to the dogs. Why don't you talk with us? We don't bite."

Judge

1. In reference to observe #7, how was the beggar's behavior wrong? Did the young man misunderstand the meaning of charity? Can you think of lessons that the beggar taught the young man about the Church's social teaching?

2. If your income decreased sharply, how would you prioritize what to do without?

3. What changes would you make to society's help for the poor?

4. Does everyone have a right to affordable housing and medical care? Why or why not?

Act

1. Go to www.nccbuscc.org/cchd/povertyusa/involved.shtml and read about how you can get involved in your community. Choose one and report back to the group on your success.

2. Using the information from the website mentioned above, return to the group with a suggestion for a group action.

3. Visit a local shelter and volunteer to help prepare and serve a meal or some other needed service. Be attentive to not just the work you may do, but also how you interact with the people you serve.

4. Make a list of all the volunteer possibilities in your community and make this available to the whole parish.

5. Organize a benefit concert involving local bands for your community food pantry. Charge a nominal fee (around $5) + a non-perishable food item for admission. Let the hall/venue know that it is a charity event to see if they will waive the fee or offer a discounted rate.

6. Organize a clothes drive at your parish to help those in need. Be sure to provide coats, hats, scarves, and gloves for the winter months.

7. Volunteer to help at a local children's home or shelter. Bring your parish youth group along and have them create games and activities for the children (i.e., play games, play music, or put on a play).

The principle of participation leads us to the conviction that the most appropriate and fundamental solutions to poverty will be those that enable people to take control of their own lives. For poverty is not merely the lack of financial resources. It entails a more profound kind of deprivation, a denial of full participation in the economic, social, and political life of society and an inability to influence decisions that affect one's life.

—US Catholic Bishops
Economic Justice for All, #188

---

5. Looking Ahead
Have a group member read aloud next week's observes on page 57. Decide together who will do which of these (you need not do them all) and share ideas about how to go about the observes.

6. Closing Prayer
Close with one of the prayers found on pages 80–82, another published prayer, or a spontaneous prayer by a member of the group.

The Dignity of Work

1. Opening Prayer

Use a prayer from pages 77–79, another published prayer, or a spontaneous prayer from a group member.

2. Report on Previous Meeting's Action

Spend a few minutes reporting on the progress of your acts from the last meeting.

3. Scriptural Reflection: *Ecclesiastes 3:9–14, Ephesians 4:28, and James 5:4*

A member of the group reads the passages aloud. All then reflect in silence or in conversation about the questions that follow it.

What is the purpose of work? How do you feel about your work? Is it simply a means of earning money, or keeping the household from falling apart? Is it rewarding in other ways?

What are the fruits of your work and how do you share them?

4. Social Inquiry: Observe, Judge, Act

Economists frequently argue that the best way to solve economic problems is to rely on the economic growth generated by each individual's pursuit of self-interest in a free market, regulated by the forces of market competition. In pursuit of income, each person provides something (product, service, or labor) that others want and are willing to pay for. Through a process of voluntary market exchange, overall production is maximized while at the same time protecting individual freedom. Since self-interest is the motor that drives the economy, incentives are all-important. The incentive of potential profit leads some people to take the risks involved in producing and marketing a new product, investing in new technologies, or lending their savings to others to do so. Other people respond to the incentive of wage differentials and undertake the training required to become a plumber, an accountant, or an engineer. Thus incentives are the key to productivity and productivity is the key to economic growth. It is efficiency, not justice, that most concerns economists.

DID YOU KNOW?

In 2009 there were more than 10 million low-income working families in the United States, an increase of nearly a quarter million from the previous year. That's nearly 1 in 3 American families touching 45 million families, including 22 million children.

In contrast, Catholic social teaching has focused on the injustices created by reliance on the free market while at the same time warning of the dangers of state socialism. In 1891 Pope Leo XIII wrote, "[T]he present age handed over the workers, each alone and defenseless, to the inhumanity of employers and the unbridled greed of competitors" (*Rerum Novarum,* #6). In 1931 Pope Pius XI wrote in *Quadragesimo Anno*, "The ultimate consequences of the individualist spirit in economic life are those which you yourselves see and deplore: free competition has destroyed itself; economic dictatorship has supplanted the free market; unbridled ambition for power has likewise succeeded greed for gain; all economic life has become tragically hard, inexorable, and cruel" (#109). In 1961 Pope John XXIII wrote in *Mater et Magistra* that because work is an expression of the human person, it can by no means be regarded as a mere commodity and that "its remuneration is not to be thought of in terms of merchandise, but rather according to the laws of justice and equity" (#18).

In 1981 Pope John Paul II wrote *Laborum Exercens* (On Human Work) because "the danger of treating work as a special kind of 'merchandise' or as an impersonal 'force' needed for production . . . always exists, especially when the whole way of looking at the question of economics is marked by the premises of materialistic economism" (*Laborum Exercens*, #7). In the encyclical, John Paul II further argues that the subjective aspect of work—its effect on the dignity of the worker—takes precedence over the objective aspect of work. That is, for example, high productivity does not compensate for or justify poor working conditions.

> The principle of the priority of labor over capital is a postulate of the order of social morality. When a person works, using all the means of production, he also wishes the fruit of this work to be used by himself and others, and he wishes to be able to take part in the very work process as a sharer in responsibility and creativity at the workbench to which he applies himself.
>
> **—Pope John Paul II**
> *Laborum Exercens*, #15

In light of economists' claims about the importance of incentives for the operation of markets, is the treatment of work in Catholic social teaching realistic? Is this "humanization" of work impossible because of (a) the way markets create a bifurcation of people as consumers/workers, coupled with the competitive pressures that force business firms to become ever more efficient; and (b) the consumerism that is rooted in human greed *and* the workings of the business system?

Because of competition, one firm can find it difficult to improve working conditions, raise wages, or democratize the workplace if the result is an increase in production costs. Competition from other firms will keep the costs from being passed on in higher prices and, thus, profits will decline. The bifurcation of people into consumers/workers means that what they prefer as consumers (lower prices) makes what they prefer as workers (better working conditions and higher wages) less obtainable. Reliance on the market as the primary decision-making mechanism splits the decision into separate areas. What people want as workers will not be ratified by those same people as consumers. Since competition is now worldwide, even a whole country faces difficulties in mandating workplace improvements that raise costs.

The problem is reinforced both by human greed and the constant effort of business to promote consumption as the ultimate end of life. This creates constant pressure to reduce labor costs, undercutting attempts to improve the quality of work life. Thus, the only hope may be to change the organization of work in ways that are both humanizing *and* efficient.

It may be that subordination of short-term interests to long-term interests and moral behavior that constrains free riding—in addition to being good in themselves—are essential for the efficient operation of the economy. Economists may be wrong when they claim that individual self-interest is sufficient to achieve efficient market outcomes. In fact, the "humanization" of work called for in Catholic social teaching may be more efficient than the present organization of work.

Consider a firm that employs workers and produces for the market. This relationship is not just a simple market relation. Unlike many markets in which the two parties enter into a transaction and that is the end of their relationship, the relationship here is very likely to be a relatively long-term one—often for a year or many years—and one in which the firm is not hiring a certain amount of labor services, but a certain number of explicit or implicit hours of labor. When the labor contract is made, the employee knows his or her wage but has not yet provided the labor services. The employer may not be able to monitor exactly how hard the employee works, especially in more complex jobs, even with supervisors, and the employee has a great deal of leeway about how much effort he or she will put into the job. The degree of effort, in turn, will depend on how the employee believes he or she is being treated by the firm. A symbol of this treatment is the wage paid to him or her, although other conditions of work also count. This can be likened to a gift exchange: if employees believe that they are being well treated and well paid, they will in return be loyal to the employer and buy into the employer's goals.

If, on the other hand, employees believe they are unfairly treated, they may not be loyal and feel no sense of duty to get the job done; they may shirk and only work the least amount that they can get away with, and may even sabotage the production process. If, however, they feel that they are treated more than fairly, they will feel satisfied with their job, proud of working for the employer, and therefore put in

DID YOU KNOW?

Forty-three percent of working families with at least one minority parent are low income, nearly twice the proportion of white working families.

a great deal of effort. If employers believe that this is the way their employees will respond, they will pay a fair wage and will try to provide a good working environment. Productivity and profits will be higher than if they did not pay a fair wage and provide for good working conditions. Moreover, there are likely to be fewer labor–firm disputes, which will have a positive effect on efficiency.

Catholic social teaching recognizes that every human being has a fundamental right to meaningful and life-sustaining work. Work not only allows people to provide for themselves and their families, but more importantly, it is a vehicle for people to carry out their God-given vocations within the world. The fact that not all people have access to work, then, is a significant flaw in our current economy. Inadequate employment is a related issue; this category includes all jobs that fail to produce adequate support of human life, whether through inadequate wages or other shortfalls.

A national unemployment rate hovering around 9 or 10 percent as we have seen over the last few years is unacceptable in light of Catholic social teaching. Many American families lack sufficient savings to subsist without employment for long. Undoubtedly, the hardest hit by economic recession are the working poor, whose jobs already pay them inadequate wages, which give them very little if anything to fall back on when their income is suddenly cut off. Unemployment can quickly lead to eviction, homelessness, and dire poverty for this sector of our society. Even for those who will not lose their homes, unemployment is a terrible blow to any family. It creates a home life full of fear and uncertainty, especially when job market prospects may well continue to be very poor for quite some time.

DID YOU KNOW?

Income inequality continues to grow with the richest 20 percent of working families taking home 47 percent of all income and earning, ten times that of low-income working families.

Unemployment, besides the obvious loss of income and financial security, has numerous negative effects on the unemployed person, not the least of which is the feeling of worthlessness that comes from being separated from the workplace. Without work, many unemployed feel out of touch with the outside world and helpless to provide an adequate standard of living for their families. The psychological damage of unemployment must not be discounted. There is substantial evidence showing that domestic violence, divorce, suicide, and the abortion rate all increase as unemployment rises.

The severe human costs of high unemployment levels become vividly clear when we examine the impact of joblessness on human lives and human dignity. It is a deep conviction of American culture that work is central to the freedom and well-being of people. The unemployed often come to feel they are worthless and without a productive role in society. Each day they are unemployed our society tells them: We don't need your talent. We don't need your initiative. We don't need you.

—US Catholic Bishops
Economic Justice for All, #141

Those who face inadequate employment also live in fear. Forced to live from paycheck to paycheck, money is a constant worry. Many take more than one job, sacrificing time with family members in order to put food on the table. Unfortunately, a number of jobs in today's economy offer no hope of advancement to better-paid positions. Particularly troubling is the situation of the worker who has been with a company for decades and still cannot afford to buy a house or a car. For these workers, the American Dream has not kept its side of the bargain. Too few businesses offer living wages, or salaries that cover all of the basic needs of the worker, and, depending on circumstances, his or her family. Workers have a right to earn enough money to provide for themselves and their dependents.

I would like to remind everyone, especially governments engaged in boosting the world's economic and social assets, that the *primary capital to be safeguarded and valued is the human person in his or her integrity.*

—Pope Benedict XVI
Caritas in Veritate, #25

We know that God loves us and cares about all aspects of our lives, including our work lives. Conditions and events at work absorb our energy, occupy our minds, and impact our psyches when we are both at work and home. Our work situations can be fulfilling and empowering, or demeaning and humiliating. Our jobs determine the size of our incomes and whether we have health insurance and a pension. Our jobs are the main determinants of whether we live in a big house or any house at all, whether we send our children to college or to bed with an empty stomach. Moreover, even at times when the economy is considered to be "strong," millions of people who want to work cannot find a job or can only find a part-time one.

Some workers confront particularly unjust situations—unsafe conditions, extremely low pay, racism, sexism, ageism, and other abuses. All workers, whatever their position in the hierarchy of jobs, may suffer from indignities, large and small, that cripple their spirit and hinder their journey to greater wholeness.

God's reign does not stop at the door to the workplace. The Church, the Body of Christ, is called to seek out and accompany people wherever they are. So the Church must also be in our offices, factories, stores, schools, and all the places where people work.

> Through the combination of social and economic change [particularly globalization], *trade union organizations* experience greater difficulty in carrying out their task of representing the interests of workers, partly because governments, for reasons of economic utility, often limit the freedom or the negotiating capacity of labor unions. Hence traditional networks of solidarity have more and more obstacles to overcome. The repeated calls issued within the Church's social doctrine, beginning with *Rerum Novarum*, for the promotion of workers' associations that can defend their rights must therefore be honored today even more than in the past, as a prompt and far-sighted response to the urgent need for new forms of

cooperation at the international level, as well as the local level.

—**Pope Benedict XVI**
Caritas in Veritate, #25

Observe

1. Ask a person who is unemployed, or has been so recently, how he or she feels about not having a job. How did it affect the family?

2. Ask several people how they feel about their work, how they are treated, how satisfied they are with the work.

3. How does your work affect your marriage and your family?

4. List the aspects of your job (and that of others in your family) that enhance human dignity and those that reduce it. Ask two friends to do the same.

What is meant by the word "decent" in regard to work? It means work that expresses the essential dignity of every man and woman in the context of their particular society: work that is freely chosen, effectively associating workers, both men and women, with the development of their community; work that enables the worker to be respected and free from any form of discrimination; work that makes it possible for families to meet their needs and provide schooling for their children, without the children themselves being forced into labor; work that permits the workers to organize themselves freely, and to make their voices heard; work that leaves enough room for rediscovering one's roots at a personal, familial and spiritual level; work that guarantees those who have retired a decent standard of living.

—Pope Benedict XVI
Caritas in Veritate, #63

Judge

1. What kind of values are embodied in the procedures, rules, promotion opportunities, and physical layout of your workplace? Do you feel they promote human dignity and the development of employees as persons?

2. In what ways do your family and job compete? What about other activities?

3. What are your views on the right of everyone to work? Would you be willing to job share?

4. Does your work serve God and further the Kingdom?

Act

1. As an individual or as a group help someone to find decent work. Make use of your access to the Internet to help them create a resume, search for job postings, and sign up for free job-search services.

2. Do something to improve your work environment so that it better supports the dignity of work and workers.

3. Before buying a product because its price is cheap try to find out the circumstances under which it was produced. Was sweatshop labor used? Is the worker being paid a fair wage?

4. Support fair trade stores and companies and businesses that treat both employees and customers with due dignity.

5. Help workers gain the skills they need to attain alternative options to minimum wage jobs. This could mean assisting them with their family responsibilities while they attend night school.

6. Avoid supporting companies that advertise in ways contrary to your beliefs. Be aware of the tendency to fall prey to consumerism and don't turn wants into "needs." Pass this on from generation to generation.

5. Looking Ahead

Have a group member read aloud next week's observes on page 68. Decide together who will do which of these (you need not do them all) and share ideas about how to go about the observes.

6. Closing Prayer

Close with one of the prayers found on pages 80–82, another published prayer, or a spontaneous prayer by a member of the group.

SESSION 7

Solidarity

1. Opening Prayer
Use a prayer from pages 77–79, another published prayer, or a spontaneous prayer from the facilitator or another group member.

2. Report on Previous Meeting's Action
Spend a few minutes reporting on the progress of your acts from the last meeting.

3. Scriptural Reflection: *Genesis 4:9–10* and *Galatians 3:26–28*
A member of the group reads the passages aloud. All then reflect in silence or in conversation.

Who are your brothers and sisters? What specifically does it mean to be their keeper in today's world? How do you try to meet this biblical mandate?

4. Social Inquiry: Observe, Judge, Act

> As society becomes ever more globalized, it makes us neighbors but does not make us brothers. Reason, by itself, is capable of grasping the equality between men and of giving stability to their civic coexistence, but it cannot establish fraternity. This originates in a transcendent vocation from God the Father, who loved us first, teaching us through the Son what fraternal charity is.
>
> **—Pope Benedict XVI**
> *Caritas in Veritate*, #19

DID YOU KNOW?

Industrialized countries account for 71 percent of global trade in consumer goods and services although they account for only 19 percent of the world's population.

We are one human family. Our responsibilities to each other cross national, racial, economic, and ideological differences. We are called to "think globally while working locally" for justice. In the economic arena as in other areas of life, competition must be complemented with cooperation. The principle of solidarity requires us to view ourselves as members of one human family. We are to see every other person as our neighbor who must share in the life to which we all are called by God. Solidarity means we are to care for our neighbors in need whether nearby or far away and to see ourselves as caretakers of our sisters and brothers in need. Catholic social teaching says that all persons, including those on the margins of society, have basic human rights necessary for integral human development, including faith and family, work and education, housing and health care.

The overriding reality of our world is the fact of interdependence among the peoples of the world. Christians have always believed that we are morally interdependent; now, since we are able to act upon it, we are morally obligated to do so.

> [Solidarity] then is not a feeling of vague compassion or shallow distress at the misfortunes of so many people, both near and far. On the contrary, it is a firm and persevering determination to commit oneself to the common good; that is to say to the good of all and of each individual, because we are all really responsible for all.
>
> The exercise of solidarity within each society is valid when its members recognize one another as persons. Those who are more influential, because they have a greater share of goods and common services, should feel responsible for the weaker and be ready to share with

them all they possess. Those who are weaker, for their part, in the same spirit of solidarity, should not adopt a purely passive attitude or one that is destructive of the social fabric, but, while claiming their legitimate rights, should do what they can for the good of all. The intermediate groups, in their turn, should not selfishly insist on their particular interests, but respect the interests of others.

—**Pope John Paul II**
Sollicitudo Rei Socialis, #38, #39

Globalization largely originates beyond the control of individual companies and countries and is nearly impossible to stop in its spread. Spurred by reduced transport costs and advances in communications and other technologies, globalization has fostered greater interdependence between the countries of the world. The resulting opportunities in international trade and foreign investment have stimulated a large and growing number of countries to liberalize their trade systems and their domestic economies. Countries that attempt to resist and instead opt for some form of isolationism risk paying a high price in economic growth. The critical question is how the aggregate gains of globalization can be translated into net benefits for the poor in the developing countries without hurting the poor in the industrial countries.

Even if the ethical considerations that currently inform debate on the social responsibility of the corporate world are not all acceptable from the perspective of the Church's social doctrine, there is nevertheless a growing conviction that business management cannot concern itself only with the interests of the proprietors, but must also assume responsibility for all the other stakeholders who contribute to the life of the business: the workers, the clients, the suppliers of various elements of production, the community of reference. In recent years a new cosmopolitan class of managers has emerged, who are often answerable only to the shareholders generally consisting of anonymous funds, which de facto determine their remuneration. By contrast, though, many far-sighted managers today are becoming increasingly aware of the profound links between their enterprise and the territory or territories in which it operates.

—Pope Benedict XVI
Caritas in Veritate, #40

Achieving the benefits and attenuating the transitional costs of globalization requires good governance within individual countries. This is dependent on the rule of law, democracy, and the provision of basic needs for the population. Without good governance, undesirable side-effects can swamp the benefits of globalization and liberalization of trade policies. Corruption, organized crime, drug trafficking, and widespread noncompliance can be the result. Good governance must develop from within the poor country itself, but international agencies, nongovernmental organizations, and countries offering aid can provide experience and advice and possibly place conditions on aid, trade, and investment aimed at promoting the common good.

Creating policies to protect people, particularly the poorest, from increased hardships is another major challenge of globalization. Public revenue and expenditure in most of Africa and Latin America have declined since the 1980s. Per capita real expenditures on basic education and health care have also fallen. In general, servicing payments on foreign and domestic debt is the primary reason for reduced public expenditures in the social sectors. These nations increasingly rely on regressive consumption taxes to generate the revenue needed to service their debt. Some countries have made major efforts to maintain social expenditures for the poor, and the World Bank has increased its

DID YOU KNOW?

The developing world spends roughly $13 on debt repayment for every dollar received in development grants.

lending to basic education and health. In addition, it has made protection of these sectors a condition of development loans. Careful attention must be paid, by poor countries, donor countries, and international agencies, to creating and supporting well-targeted social programs.

While globalization can bring increased productivity to developing nations and improve the condition of their poor, there is no guarantee that it will automatically happen. International streams of finance, investment, and goods are notoriously unstable, and as countries liberalize trade and commerce, they become more susceptible to these instabilities. A more effective worldwide institutional framework for oversight, regulation, and compensation is necessary to deal with shocks emanating from the volatility of short-term international financial flows.

Further debt reduction/forgiveness is necessary to reduce the debt servicing obligations of the least developed countries, particularly in Africa. Such reductions would free up budgetary resources for use elsewhere. As a requirement of debt forgiveness, creditor countries could insist that the released resources be used for basic education, health care, and nutrition.

The globalization of international markets and of the various national economies means that individual policies regarding exchange rates, trade, capital flows, and debt will be more effective if set within supra-national programs that encourage and coordinate them. Just as it has been necessary for all countries, developed and undeveloped alike, to introduce various measures to control the workings of their domestic economies for the common good, it may be essential to extend those measures to the international economy.

The principle of social solidarity suggests that alleviating poverty will require fundamental changes in social and economic structures that perpetuate glaring inequalities and cut off millions of citizens from full participation in the economic and social life of the nation. The process of change should be one that draws together all citizens, whatever their economic status, into one community.

—US Catholic Bishops
Economic Justice for All, #187

Another reality of the world economy is that different countries have different policies toward issues that impact international prices, minimum wages, environmental protection, and antitrust laws. For example, if the United States has child labor laws, a minimum wage, other social benefits such as social security and unemployment benefits, and environmental regulations, its costs of production will be higher, and thus less competitive, than a country that does not have them. A simple multilateral free trade policy places enormous pressure on the United States to undermine these social regulations. We cannot stop the changes that are spreading through the world economy. We cannot build a "Fortress America" against the rest of the world. It will not work. And we shouldn't want it to. Other peoples' welfare must figure into our decisions.

A key problem for the United States then is negotiating transitional adjustments to soften human suffering. In those cases of massive dislocation, trade readjustment aid needs to be increased. Retraining programs for displaced workers, relocation allowances, and subsidies will help the impacted communities attract new businesses, in addition to increasing economic efficiency by providing access to new skills and encouraging mobility of resources.

The key issue here is that worker retraining and relocation, community investment, and other policies are necessary if we want to *manage the transition* from an industrial to post-industrial economy. Similar transitions in the past were, by default, paid for by the people and communities left behind by the creative-destructive processes of capitalist development. The question is not whether we must make the transition but how—and how to do so while respecting the rights of people, particularly the poorest. In *Economic Justice for All* the US Bishops argue that the principle of solidarity requires the United States to lower import barriers to products made in poor countries even if this results in increased unemployment here. The reasoning behind this challenge is that as a richer country, the United-ed States can afford to retrain and help workers and businesses to re-locate more easily than developing nations can (#251–292). Such are the challenges that Catholic social teaching poses.

DID YOU KNOW?

For the 10 years from 1994 to 2004, the US Department of Labor certified for Trade Adjustment Assistance more than 1.35 million workers who lost their jobs due to changes in international trade. For the single year 2010, the number of workers certified had climbed to over 280,000.

Pope John Paul II argues that there must be social intervention on the international level "to pro-mote development, an effort which also involves sacrificing the posi-tions of income and power enjoyed by the more developed countries" (*Centesimus Annus*, #52). To carry out this effort, "it is not enough to draw on the surplus goods which in fact our world abundantly pro-duces: it requires above all a change of life-styles, of models of production and consumption, and of the established structures of power which today govern societies" (*Centesimus Annus*, #58). He goes on to say, "This increasing internationalization of the economy ought to be accompanied by effective international agencies which will oversee and direct the economy to the common good, some-thing that an individual state, even if it were the most powerful on earth, would not be in a position to do" (*Centesimus Annus*, #58).

We are our brothers' and sisters' keepers, wherever they live. We are one human family, whatever our national, racial, ethnic, economic, and ideological differences. Learning to practice the virtue of solidarity means learning that "loving

our neighbor" has global dimensions in an interdependent
world.

—US Catholic Bishops
Sharing Catholic Social Teaching

Observe

1. Think of a personal experience in which following the principle of solidarity allowed you to accomplish something. Relate this experience to the group.

2. Are there newcomers to your community, such as immigrants? How are they received in the community? Check with the local Catholic Charities for information.

3. Ask the grocer in your local supermarket where various produce items were grown. Research the economic and social conditions for workers in those places.

4. Have one group member investigate working conditions and child labor practices in a country such as China or India.

5. Check to see if the jobs that disappeared in your community did so because of competition from abroad.

Judge

1. Is your community divided along ethnic, racial, economic, or other lines? How would you judge this in the light of the principle of solidarity?

2. In what ways is your life affected by the global economy both positively and negatively?

3. What barriers have to be overcome before people from different groups can productively work together?

4. Has your community been enriched by new ethnic groups moving into the area? If so, in what specific ways?

5. What obligations do you have to know the labor practices of the companies you buy from and of their subcontractors around the world?

Act

1. See what assistance you can offer to local groups helping new immigrants adapt to your area. For those that are undocumented, explore ways that you can help safeguard their dignity.

2. Working through your parish, set up a meeting with Protestant and non-Christian groups that are working to solve similar problems. Address issues such as immigration and the working poor. Join with them and work toward a common goal, learning from each other along the way.

3. Find out what retraining and relocation funds are available for workers in your community displaced by foreign competition. Contact your congressional representative urging them to support such legislation.

4. Learn about the culture of immigrant groups in your area. Encourage your neighbors to hold onto their culture by showing interest in their religious practices and celebrations as well as other cultural activities important to them.

5. Explore government policies on minimum wage and "living wage" proposals. How do these policies affect the working poor? What standards should the government set to ensure that workers are compensated adequately for the work they do? Let your opinions be known to local government officials.

6. Learn a new language. If practical, make it a language that is spoken by immigrants in your area. This will allow you to sympathize with immigrants who struggle to learn English while helping make you better qualified for many jobs that could benefit the community.

7. Adopt a "sister" parish from a neighboring town in your area that has a different ethnic background than yours. Share your customs and traditions with each other. Include each other in

parish activities and incorporate foods from a variety of local cultures at parish gatherings.

5. Looking Ahead
Have a group member read aloud next week's observes on page 74. Then decide together who will do which of these (you need not do them all) and share ideas about how to go about the observes.

6. Closing Prayer
Close with one of the prayers found on pages 80–82, another published prayer, or a spontaneous prayer by a member of the group.

For the Lord your God is God of gods and Lord of lords, the great God, mighty and awesome, who is not partial and takes no bribe, who executes justice for the orphan and the widow, and who loves the strangers, providing them with food and clothing. You shall also love the stranger, for you were strangers in the land of Egypt.

—Deuteronomy 10:17–19

Subsidiarity

1. Opening Prayer
Use a prayer from pages 77–79, another published prayer, or a spontaneous prayer from a group member.

2. Report on Previous Meeting's Action
Spend a few minutes reporting on the progress of your acts from the last meeting.

3. Scriptural Reflection: *Luke 10:25–37*
A member of the group reads the passage aloud. All then reflect in silence or in conversation.

If this situation occurred today in your town or city, what do you expect would be the response? How willing would you be to get involved and take care of everything yourself like the Samaritan did?

4. Social Inquiry: Observe, Judge, Act

Solutions to our economic problems will be found only if citizens are willing to cooperate in the difficult adjustments necessary to change the economy and build a new social consensus. This requires policies to be developed and implemented at the lowest feasible levels—an embodiment of the principle of subsidiarity.

The principle of subsidiarity is built upon the understanding that we have a pluralism of social actors, where each has certain obligations. Higher levels should not usurp the authority of lower levels except when necessary. And conversely, when lower levels cannot meet social obligations, higher levels of social actors must step in. As pointed out in the first session, when individuals, families, or

DID YOU KNOW?

On September 28, 2010, Sen. Robert P. Casey (D-PA) and Rep. James McGovern (D-MA) introduced the National Opportunity and Community Renewal Act, S. 3845/H.R. 6222, a culmination of 12 months of work by Catholic Charities USA to identify innovative strategies existing in communities throughout the country that will serve to revamp our nation's approach to poverty prevention and alleviation.

local communities are not able to solve problems that undermine the common good, state governments are obligated to intervene, and if their resources and abilities are not sufficient, the federal government must assume responsibility. The same principle extends to the international community.

Less than half of the eligible electorate bothers to vote in a typical US election. Yet, there has been a proliferation of neighborhood groups and other small local organizations. National institutions may have become too large, too uncontrollable, and too unresponsive. Catholic social teaching supports the development of smaller organizations that are closer and more responsive to local needs. These groupings naturally evolve out of the interactions of people in their day-by-day activities. These range from the Knights of Columbus and the Elks, to parish food pantries and Goodwill Industries, to not-for-profit hospitals and private colleges and universities. These and a myriad of other such organizations make up what is called civil society. These interact with and temper the actions of the for-profit sector and the state sector (made up of all the levels of government).

> As history abundantly proves, it is true that on account of changed conditions many things which were done by small associations in former times cannot be done now save by large associations. Still, that most weighty principle, which cannot be set aside or changed, remains fixed and unshaken in social philosophy: Just as it is gravely wrong to take from individuals what they can

accomplish by their own initiative and industry and give it to the community, so also it is an injustice and at the same time a grave evil and disturbance of right order to assign to a greater and higher association what lesser and subordinate organizations can do. For every social activity ought of its very nature to furnish help to the members of the body social, and never destroy and absorb them.

—**Pope Pius XI**
Quadragesimo Anno, #79–#80

US society today is characterized by largeness of firms and government institutions. Exxon Mobil, Chase Bank, and IBM are all mega institutions. Government agencies such as the Department of Defense are even larger. The development of the US economy has created a fundamental division of social, political, and economic life. Put most simply, the dichotomy is between the mega institutions and the pri-

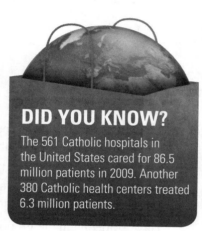

DID YOU KNOW?

The 561 Catholic hospitals in the United States cared for 86.5 million patients in 2009. Another 380 Catholic health centers treated 6.3 million patients.

vate life of the individual. People could cope with these mega institutions better if the process had not so deinstitutionalized their private life. People have always found their identity through and, in turn, impressed their values on the mega institutions through what are called "mediating structures." This is where freedom is nurtured and protected, where the counter to bureaucracy lies, where moral values can play a role in resource allocation. However, this interlocking network of mediating institutions—family, church, voluntary associations, neighborhoods, and social subcultures—has been severely weakened by the growth of the mega institutions that have taken over many of the traditional functions of these smaller institutions.

Subsidiarity respects personal dignity by recognizing in the person a subject who is always capable of giving something to others. By considering reciprocity as the heart of what it is to be a human being, subsidiarity is the most effective antidote against any form of all-encompassing welfare state.

The principle of subsidiarity must remain closely linked to the principle of solidarity and vice versa, since the former without the latter gives way to social privatism, while the latter without the former gives way to paternalist social assistance that is demeaning to those in need.

—**Pope Benedict XVI**
Caritas in Veritate, #57, #58

Observe

1. Make a list of successful local groups in your community that embody the principle of subsidiarity.

2. Find out if your local parish has a program to help the poor and disadvantaged. If they do, ask how they think they do a better job than a larger organization, such as the city or county.

3. Have someone in the group ask an official in local government what they do well and why they think they can do it better than the state government.

Judge

1. In your experience, what products and services are best delivered by local groups? How do these groups and the services they provide embody the principle of subsidiarity?

2. What products and services do you think are best delivered by your state government? How does it embody the principle of subsidiarity?

3. What products and services do you think are best delivered by the federal government? How does it embody the principle of subsidiarity?

4. Are there products or services that need to be delivered by an international authority?

Act

1. Ask your local congressional representative to explain his or her view of subsidiarity in the political sphere. Get involved in local politics, encouraging government officials to take care of the community they represent.

2. Examine the effectiveness of private charities versus government programs in truly helping the poor with particular need. Ask yourself whether your money and/or your time is put to better use by contributions to a political party or cause or a private charity or social service organization (Catholic Charities, Society of St. Vincent de Paul, Knights of Columbus, etc.). Decide which sector does a better job in helping the poor with this particular need and give accordingly.

3. Find out where your supermarket buys its produce and research the pros and cons of that system. Consider environmental and human costs at all levels of the system. Decide how you want to respond to this consumption pattern.

4. Find out if there is a local food cooperative. Is buying from local sources a better option for you and your family? Why or why not?

5. Contact your local Catholic Charities office to seek out volunteer opportunities.
www.catholiccharitiesusa.org/NetCommunity/

6. Contact your local Society of St. Vincent de Paul or Catholic Worker to offer your financial support. Volunteer to help with the poor, the shut-ins, the elderly, and the orphaned.
www.svdpusa.org/Home.aspx

5. Looking Ahead
Have a brief discussion about what will be your next steps as individuals or perhaps as a group. What have you learned and what will you do with that knowledge?

6. Closing Prayer
Close with one of the prayers found on pages 80–82, another published prayer, or a spontaneous prayer by a member of the group.

Opening Prayers

Almighty and eternal God,

May your grace enkindle in all a love for the
    many unfortunate people whom poverty
    and misery reduce to a condition unworthy
    of human beings.

Arouse in the hearts of those who call you,
    Father, a hunger and thirst for social jus-
    tice and for fraternal charity in deeds and
    truth.

Grant, O Lord, peace in our days,
    peace to souls, peace to families,
    peace to our country, peace among nations.

Amen.

—From the Holy Year Prayer of Pope Pius XII

Gracious God,

Strengthen us with humility and wisdom.
Teach us to be thankful for the precious mys-
    tery of life that you have made ours. Bless
    our efforts to promote the total develop-
    ment of each and every human being
    that all might reach the fullness of their
    potential and dignity as your sons and
    daughters.
Amen.

— Adapted from a prayer by Cardinal Terence Cooke,
Archbishop of New York, 1968–1983

Father,

Send in your name the Holy Spirit
who will teach us everything,
who will remind us of every word of Jesus,
    who will stay with us forever.
The Spirit will console us,
the Spirit will sustain us
along the difficult paths of the world,
the Spirit will lead us to truth
in order to be true in love.
The Spirit will open us to future things,
the Spirit will give us what is
of the Father and of the Son.
Father,
may your Spirit fill the life of each of us,
may your Spirit fill our hearts,
may our community overflow with love,
may prophets arise, may dreams grow,
may mercy spring forth,
may your Spirit flow throughout the world,
may your Spirit blow where he wants,
especially where there is sorrow, loneliness,
    and cold,
may your Spirit renew the face of all men and
    women,
renew the hearts of the people,
change the earth.
With faith, with one heart,
Father, we invoke you.
Amen.

—*The Sant' Egidio Book of Prayer*, pp. 178–197

Closing Prayers

My soul magnifies the Lord,
and my spirit rejoices in God my Savior,
for he has looked with favor on the lowliness
    of his servant.
Surely, from now on all generations will call
    me blessed;
for the Mighty One has done great things for
    me,
and holy is his name.
His mercy is for those who fear him
from generation to generation.
He has shown strength with his arm;
he has scattered the proud in the thoughts of
    their hearts.
He has brought down the powerful from their
    thrones,
and lifted up the lowly;
he has filled the hungry with good things,
and sent the rich away empty.
He has helped his servant Israel,
in remembrance of his mercy,
according to the promise he made to our
    ancestors,
to Abraham and to his descendants forever.

—Luke 1:46–55

All: Justice shall flourish in his time,
and fullness of peace forever.

Rdr: Justice shall flower in his days,
and profound peace, till the moon be no
more.
May he rule from sea to sea,
and from the River to the ends of the
earth.

All: Justice shall flourish in his time, and
fullness of peace forever.

Rdr: For he shall rescue the poor when they
cry out,

and the afflicted when they have no one
to help.
He shall have pity for the lowly and the
poor,
the lives of the poor he shall save.

All: Justice shall flourish in his time, and
fullness of peace forever.

Rdr: May his name be blessed forever;
as long as the sun his name shall remain.
In him shall all the tribes of the earth be
blessed;
all nations shall proclaim his happiness!

All: Justice shall flourish in his time, and
fullness of peace forever.

—Psalm 72:7–8, 12–13, 17

Lord, make me an instrument of your peace.

Where there is hatred, let me sow love;
where there is injury, pardon;
where there is doubt, faith;
where there is despair, hope;
where there is darkness, light;
and where there is sadness, joy.
O Divine Master, grant that I may not so much
    seek
to be consoled as to console;
to be understood as to understand;
to be loved as to love.
For it is in giving that we receive;
it is in pardoning that we are pardoned;
and it is in dying that we are born to eternal
    life. Amen.

—Peace Prayer of Saint Francis of Assisi

Charles K. Wilber is the emeritus professor of economics at the University of Notre Dame and a fellow of the Joan B. Kroc Institute for International Peace Studies. He served as economic adviser to the United States Conference of Catholic Bishops for their 1986 pastoral letter, *Economic Justice for All*. Wilber has written or edited over a dozen books and published numerous articles, including several in *National Catholic Reporter*, *Commonweal*, *Preach*, and *America*. He has been married to Mary Ellen Wilber for over fifty years. Together they have long been active in faith-sharing groups such as the Christian Family Movement, and have raised seven children.

Founded in 1865, Ave Maria Press,
a ministry of the Congregation of
Holy Cross, is a Catholic publishing
company that serves the spiritual and
formative needs of the Church and its
schools, institutions, and ministers;
Christian individuals and families; and
others seeking spiritual nourishment.

For a complete listing of titles from

Ave Maria Press

Sorin Books

Forest of Peace

Christian Classics

visit www.avemariapress.com

ave maria press® / Notre Dame, IN 46556
A Ministry of the United States Province of Holy Cross